WOLVENDAUGHTER

CREATED BY
VER

LETTERED BY
EVE GREENWOOD

EDITED BY
EVE GREENWOOD
& ALEX ASSAN

FIRST EDITION © 2021 VER
PUBLISHED BY QUINDRIE PRESS
QUINDRIEPRESS.COM

ISBN 9781914548000

QUINDRIE
PRESS

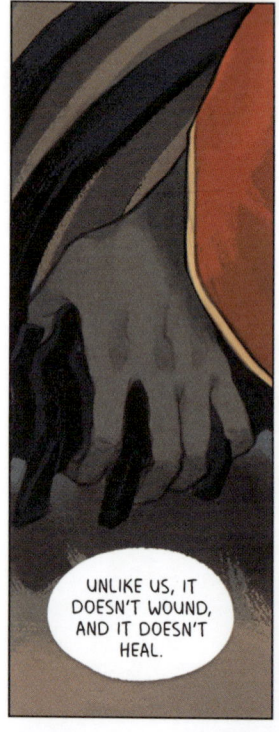

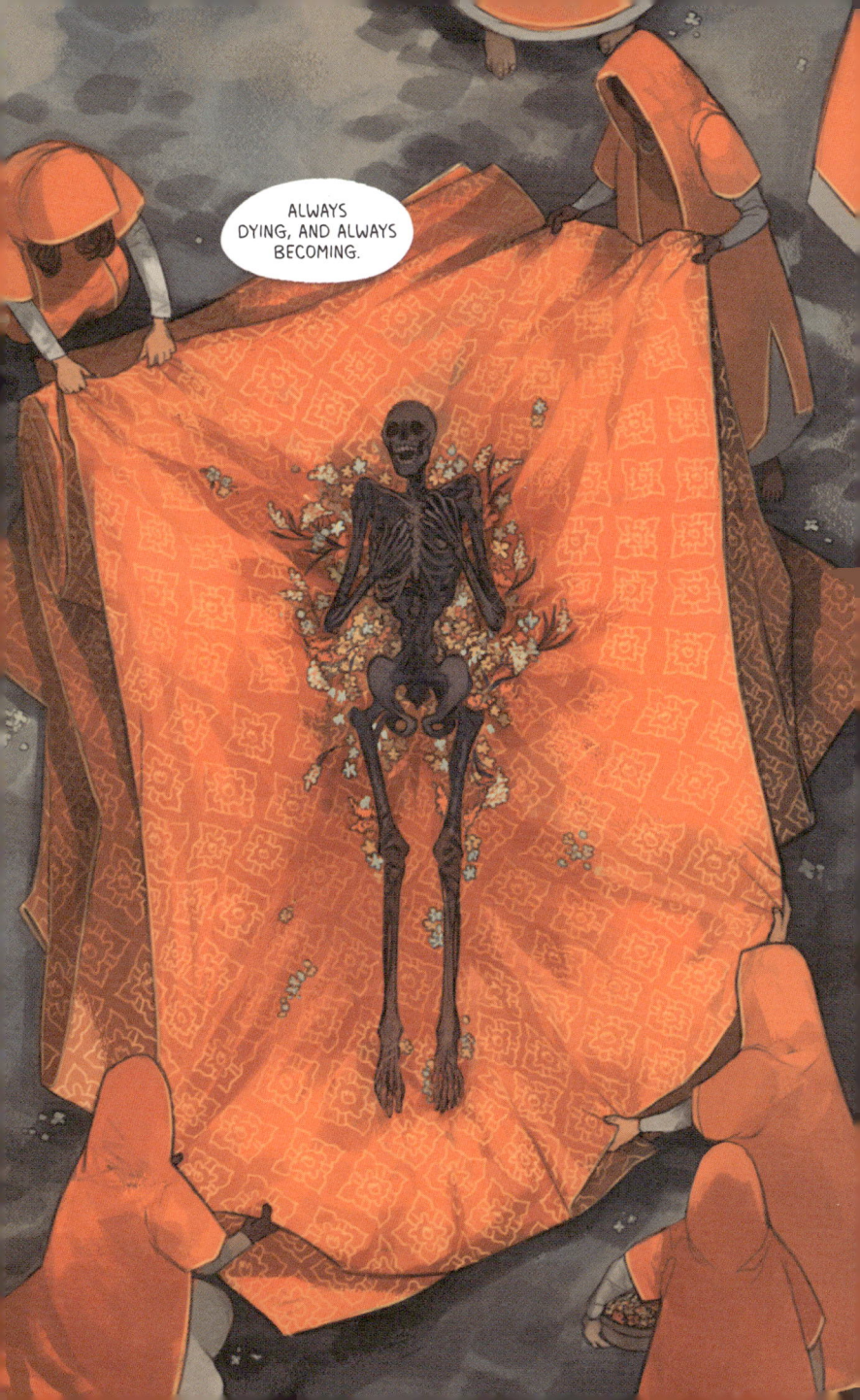

REMEMBER THE GENTLE TOUCH OF GRASS BENEATH YOUR FEET, AND HOLD THAT MEMORY DEAR.

REMEMBER THE BLUE SKIES, AND THE TURN OF SEASONS AS THEY ONCE WERE.

AND REMEMBER THE KINDNESS PEOPLE ONCE SHOWED YOU, AS THEY WILL HOLD NO LOVE FOR YOU NOW.

H—

KH—

H—

H—

H—

SNAP!

CHOKING ON HOPE UNTIL THE FLAME BURNED ITSELF OUT.

WITH NO BEAST IN SIGHT, AND ONLY THE DAUGHTER TO BLAME.

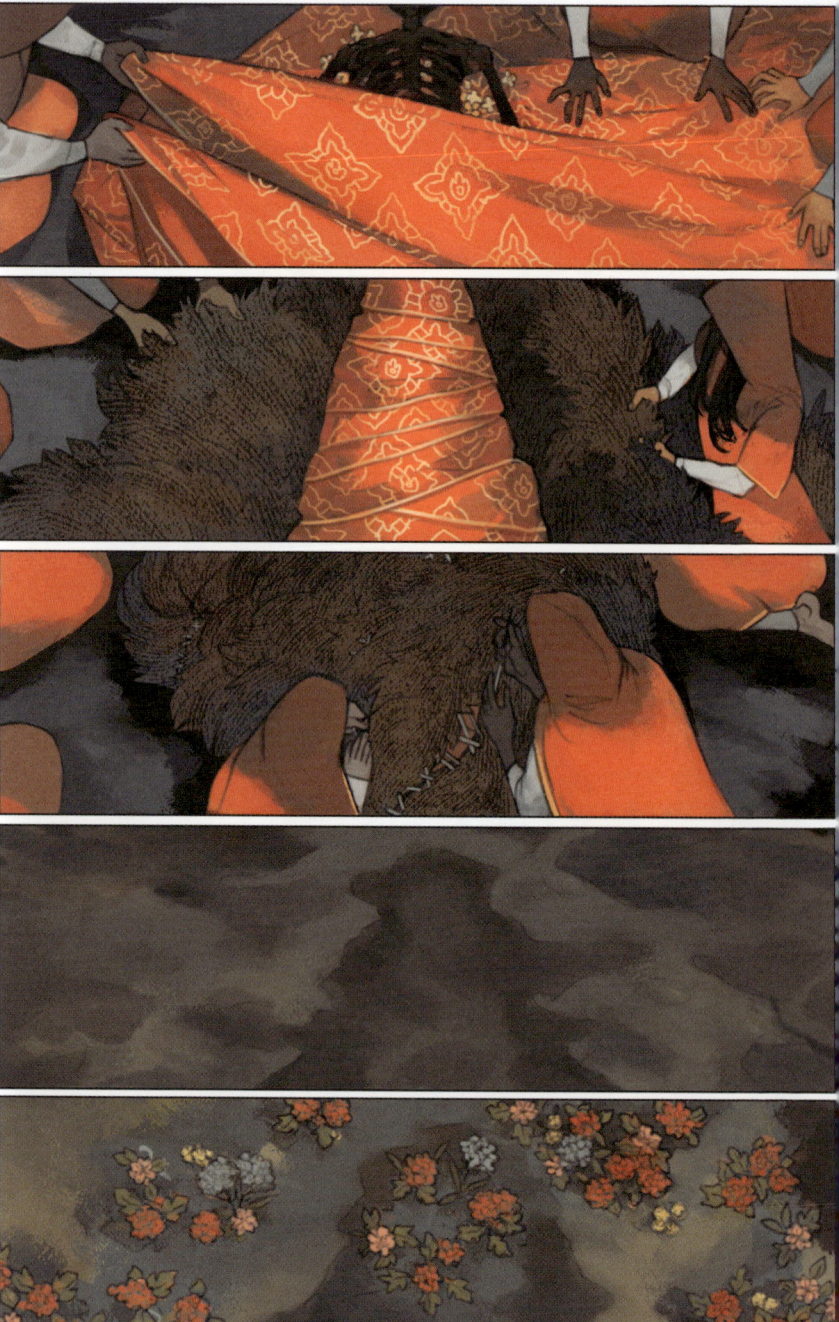

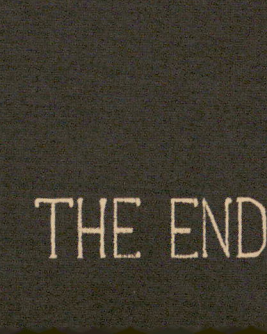

THE END

ABOUT THE AUTHOR

VER

Ver is a writer and illustrator from Eastern Europe
residing in Scotland. They spend most of their
time writing and drawing stories about strange
people and distant worlds.

 VERFACE